ADVENTURE

by

Jay Eiger

WWW.OAKLEAPRESS.COM

ADVENTURE © 2023 by Edward M LLC. All rights reserved. No part of this book may be used or reproduced in any manner whatsoever without written permission except in the case of brief quotations embodied in critical articles and reviews. For information visit:

www.OakleaPress.com

Table of Contents

Foreword 5
Part One: My Journey to Europe 7
    Introduction
    Growing Up and Going to College
    How the Plan to Travel to Europe Was Hatched
    Graduation Rolls Around
    Back Home in Richmond
    Leaving Home for Parts Unknown
    Life About the Ship
    The Canaries and Gibraltar
    We Arrive at Barcelona
Part Two: Barcelona, Alicante, & Madrid 31
    Barcelona
    Alicante and the East Coast of Spain
    Madrid, a Beautiful City and a Bullfight
Part Three: Séte, Nice, Monte Carlo 45
    We Think We're Headed to Nice
    An Evening on the Beach
    Monte Carlo
    We Say "Au Revoir" to the French Girls
Part Four: Rome, Florence & Venice 57
    Bob and I Travel to Rome
    We Go to Florence
    We Go to Venice
Part Five: Salzburg, Grindelwald, Germany,
Norway, Amsterdam 75
    Salzburg
    Switzerland and the Eiger
    Another Serendipity

Contents

    The Eiger
    We Go to Germany
    Norway Came Next
    Did Someone Say, "Red Light District?"
    A Night in Amsterdam
Part Six: Paris & Dover 101
    Paris When It Sizzles
    We Meet Two French Girls
    We Fly Ten Feet High to London
Part Seven: Edinburgh & London 115
    Edinburgh, Scotland
    Back to London
    The Alabama Ladies
    The Tower of London
    The Hard Rock Cafe
    The Grenadier Pub
    The RAF Club
Part Eight: Home Again, Home Again 131
    My First Real Flight
    A Hero's Journey
    Home Was Not So Sweet
Epilogue 137

Foreword

When contemplating this book, I really had to dig deep for memories. I believe that taking many pictures and protecting them since 1977 helped with this, as well as having a good memory.

What started as a thought one night at a southern university in the winter of 1977 turned into a wonderful, fun and enlightening adventure that a lot of today's 21 year olds may never experience. The Eurail pass was a great invention. You could purchase one in the United States for $175 back then (today one costs around $750) and ride anywhere by simply jumping on a train. To me, it was truly unbelievable.

My buddy Bob and I definitely wanted to experience the culture of each city as well as churches, museums, historic buildings, and the different food in each country as we traveled. We were 21, and we obviously wanted to meet up with girls along the way. Well, we were definitely successful in both areas as you will see as you read ahead.

The excitement, enlightenment, and fun were out of this world. I hope you experience some of that as you read my true adventure story.

         Jay Eiger
         April 2023

"A mind that is stretched by a new experience can never go back to its old dimensions."

– Oliver Wendell Holmes

Part One: My Journey to Europe

Introduction

I was born in the mid 1950s and raised in the Southeast, in a world very different from today's. It was a time when, for most, college was affordable—few, if any, were burdened with debt after graduation. The Cold War may have been raging, but even so, it was an idyllic time. Unlike today, politics was far from our minds. We could express our thoughts and feelings honestly—and no one judged. Jobs were plentiful and thousands took a few months after graduation to travel to and around Europe—carrying backpacks, sleeping bags, and staying in youth hostels. I was one of them. It was an extraordinary adventure still vivid in my mind that I want to tell you about.

Growing Up and Going to College

I was accepted by two colleges in the Southeast, both of which were still all male back then, and a university that was co-ed. After visiting the all-male colleges, it occurred to me I'd prefer to spend the next four years in one where there'd be women around so I decided on the university.

I joined a fraternity and made friends—many who are still friends today. The largest group—about 60%—was from Lookout Mountain, Tennessee. From there, the membership was scattered—three from Richmond, a few others from Charleston, South Carolina, Atlanta, and smaller cities and towns in the Southeast.

At that time, there weren't many places to go in our college town, and so the social life of the university revolved around fraternities and sororities. We would invite the members of other fraternities to join us for parties at our house, and they would reciprocate. As you might suspect, there were a lot of parties—it was a friendly and cordial time—so much so that I had to force myself to make time and to take time to study. But I managed to make it to all my classes and to graduate with a 2.8 GPA. Fortunately, it was a time when employers were more interested in who you were as an individual more so than your GPA or your college transcripts. For most of us, getting that first job was not particularly difficult.

Although I was a marketing management major, I was influenced to take a different path by a finance professor who had worked at Merrill Lynch in New York. A very bright guy, on the first day of his class he said, "We are not going to talk about accounting. You can learn about that in your accounting class. We are going to study the markets. You will learn about the United States markets and the global markets, and you will learn how to invest and what to invest in."

He and that class had a big effect on me. Instead of marketing, I went into finance, and I'll say with some humility that it was the right decision for me. Besides that decision, and the trip to Europe you will soon read about, the people around me helped make me who I am. They were not judgmental—not about anything. They simply wanted to enjoy themselves and get to know others.

Adventure

I have to admit, it was not unusual for us to do nutty things. For example, one day, a fraternity brother and I each got a six-pack of beer and boarded the bus that went all around campus. We thought we'd meet some girls. We didn't, but at least we gave it the college try.

When I think about the academics and classes I took, the one that comes to mind first, besides that finance class, was one I took in the business school. It was a statistics class, and it was hard. The professor was about 70 years old, maybe older, and he'd been teaching a long time. Most of what we were supposed to learn went right over my head. In the end, he gave me and someone else who was not doing well C-minuses. I think the professor felt sorry for us. He must have realized that without that credit, we were not going to graduate.

Thank goodness he had mercy on us.

How the Plan to Travel to Europe Was Hatched

The plan to backpack through Europe was hatched sometime during the winter of my senior year. We had a fireplace in the basement of the Fraternity house, and we were having a few drinks, enjoying the fire one evening, chewing the fat, when we started talking about what we were going to do after graduation. I recall that I was sipping Scotch—Usher's Green Stripe—about the cheapest brand you can buy—one guaranteed to produce a powerful hangover. Whatever the case may be, with the fire going full blast, and six of us settled in, one of the brothers took a sip and said, "You know,

Adventure

I don't want to go straight to work. I want to do something fun, first—before I settle down for the rest of my life. If I don't do it now, I never will."

Everyone nodded in agreement.

Another brother said, "Look, I've got a sailboat. It's a 30-foot Bristol. We could sail around the Caribbean. Heck, we could sail around the world."

After some discussion, the consensus was that that idea was probably not a good one. The boat wasn't big enough.

Then another good friend spoke up. I will not use his real name because he would rather remain anonymous—I'll call him "Bob." Anyway, Bob said, "My father's an executive at a company that ships a product all over the world. He knows the head of distribution. I'll bet he could get us a job on a freighter. We could go to Europe, and we wouldn't have to pay anything to get there."

I said, "Bob, that is a fantastic idea. You need to look into that."

Well, Bob did look into it, and his dad found us jobs on a Norwegian freighter, and with those jobs, free passage to Europe. The ship was scheduled to sail on June 12, bound for Barcelona. All we had to do was show up at the freighter at Port Newark, New Jersey.

I have to say the idea of taking a freighter to Europe was mind-blowing. I'd never seen a freighter, much less been on one. Heck, I'd never been out of Richmond, except to the Carolina beaches and to college, which by itself was an eye-opener—a university with 26,000 students, more than half of whom were

Adventure

attractive women. But there was much more to come—many more eye-openers.

Graduation Rolls Around

That conversation in the basement of the fraternity house took place not long before I finished. The university was on a quarter system, and I graduated at the end of the winter quarter—right before the spring quarter of 1977. I decided to spend March, April, and May in Hilton Head because I was pretty sure that's where I could make some extra cash to increase the amount of money I had set aside for my trip to Europe. You see, I'd spent summers in college in Nags Head, North Carolina. My parents paid my college tuition and my fraternity dues, and I was able to earn and save all the spending money I needed—surfing during the day and waiting tables at night. I'd rake in up to $150 in tips and put it in the bank each morning.

So that's what I did. I waited tables at the Hilton Head Inn. As had been the case in Nags Head, it was possible to make well over a hundred dollars a night in tips, and so that's how I earned the extra money I needed to finance my trip while having a good time doing it. Looking back, I was the only white person on the wait staff. Everyone else was black—all of them terrific guys. We had a lot of fun—I miss them and feel a sense of nostalgia when I think about that time.

At the end of May, I left Hilton Head, headed up the coast, and stopped off at Nags Head. I knew several girls working there who went to Mary Baldwin and Hollins. I went out with one of them, and we hit it off—

Adventure

there was chemistry between us. Unfortunately, I was only able to stay two or three days. I had to leave in order to meet my friend and head to Europe. I also knew that when I returned from Europe, she'd be away on a junior year abroad. But that was not the end of our relationship, or our romance.

When she returned from France, we dated for two years.

Back Home

When I got back home, I spent a few days going to a friends pool, seeing some old friends and packing up to go to Europe for three months. Then, Bob and I boarded an Amtrak train for New Jersey. It was the first week in June and already hot and humid in my home town. I recall feeling the heat, the heavy air, and the smell of diesel fuel as we climbed on board.

Port Newark, New Jersey

Leaving Home for Parts Unknown

We slept on the train. It was a little uncomfortable, but we managed, and it didn't seem long before we arrived at Port Newark. It was a hot, summer day, and the sun beat down on all kinds of freighters—they were everywhere we looked, most of them scruffy and rundown.

Our ship, however, was a pleasant surprise. A Norwegian vessel, a huge ship about 500 feet long—I was struck by the immense size of it, and that it, unlike most of the other ships in the harbor, was clean and well kept—freshly painted. The captain greeted us dressed in his all-white uniform decked out with epaulets on his shoulders. He was a true gentleman—a Norwegian who spoke perfect English.

He looked at Bob and said, "Your father's colleague was in touch with me. We do have room, and that is why you are here. You will be termed 'work-a-way sailors.' You will not be paid, but you will have a job, and you will work every day. We are going first to the Canary Islands, and you will be able to get off the ship and travel around for a day or two. We will then pass through the Strait of Gibraltar, and on to Barcelona where you will disembark."

We didn't know what our jobs would be, but we didn't care. We said, "Great! Terrific! Sounds good."

Then the captain showed us to our quarters. I was a little surprised to find that we each had our own berth.

We're on the way!

Life Aboard the Ship

Not much happened that first afternoon. The ship was being loaded, mostly with containers and there wasn't much that we could do to help. Then I recall being called to dinner, which took place in a galley that accommodated about 20 people. Not everyone ate at the same time. The crew numbered about 30 in total, and some worked while others ate.

One thing that I found remarkable was the Norwegian diet. It was very protein-driven—a lot of salmon and other fish, eggs, fruit, some beef. In my opinion, it's very healthy, and so I still adhere to that diet today.

Tired from the overnight train trip from Richmond, I got a good night's sleep that first night. The next morning, there was a knock on the door from one of our shipmates, "6:30, 6:30, time to get up!"

I put on my most ragged clothes—cut off khaki shorts, an old t-shirt from years before that I didn't care about. We had breakfast and then started chipping paint off the deck of the ship with chisel hammers. That took some getting used to. It was necessary to bear down on those pneumatic hammers for them to work as intended. They were like miniature jackhammers that shook your whole body.

We were the only crewmembers with that particular job assignment, and so chipping paint is what we did all day, every day. After a few days I guess we pretty much got used to it. As you can imagine, it was gritty, and grimy chipping paint, and that's what we got—gritty and grimy. Fortunately, every berth had a shower,

Adventure

Sunset on the ocean

a pretty good one. We took at least one every day, but we never washed those shorts and t-shirts. We knew we were going to throw them away at the end of the trip. It was hard work, and I can honestly say, I never had trouble sleeping at night.

Each berth had a porthole. I kept mine open and there was always a breeze—we didn't have air conditioning, and we didn't need it. The temperature was perfect. I was always exhausted at the end of the day. In no time at all, the motion of the ship on the ocean rocked me to sleep every night. I don't think I have ever slept more soundly—either before or since.

It had been hot and humid in Richmond and hot in Newark, but it wasn't hot out on the ocean. There always seemed to be a breeze. Nevertheless, it was important to use plenty of sunscreen—the sun was intense.

I have to say that it's really special being out there—with nothing but water all the way to the horizon in whatever direction you looked. One thing that amazed me was the color of the water. It was deep, deep blue—Navy blue. No wonder that's what that shade of blue is called. And, as you may have seen in movies, porpoises really did track alongside the boat. It appeared to be like a game for them—they seemed to love to keep up with us, and show off their swimming prowess.

We also saw some sharks—big ones.

Something else that was impressive—sunrises and sunsets when you are out in the middle of the ocean are awe inspiring, as is the ocean at night—the great arch of sky with incredibly bright stars and moon is

Dressed for work
(Bob wants to remain anonymous, hence the mask over his face.)

something to behold. There is absolutely no light pollution, and for a moment, or a few minutes, you feel yourself in touch with—perhaps even overwhelmed by—eternity.

The only other man-made object we saw during the twelve-day journey between Newark and the Canary Islands was a small sailboat—probably 30 feet long. It happened during a storm. There were two guys on it, sailing from Bristol to Cape Cod. They came right alongside our ship.

I yelled down to them, "Are you guys going to be okay?!"

"Yeah," they yelled back. "We do this all the time—it's no big deal!"

Actually, the weather was pretty good for most of the trip. It rained a couple of times, and we went through a squall that lasted maybe eight hours. It was a roller coaster ride—way, way up, and way, way down, waves crashing over the deck. You felt the bottom of your stomach fall away—like on a fast-starting elevator ride. Even so, I don't recall ever being afraid, or worrying about being out in the middle of nowhere, thousands of miles from land. That simply did not occur to me.

And I never got seasick.

Bob, however, did get seasick fairly often, depending on the weather and how it affected the motion of the ship. Sometimes, while we were chipping paint, and the sea was somewhat rough, I'd look over at him, and he seemed to be turning pale green. I'd tell him he needed to go to his berth and lie down.

Life below deck

Adventure

There was a boatswain, or petty officer, also known as a "deck boss," who was in charge of us and the rest of the crew. When Bob had to go below, I'd explain, partially using sign language, that Bob was seasick and had to go lie down. The guy would just smile knowingly and nod. He was a Norwegian with red hair who would have been cast in a movie as the stereotypical Viking—a big guy with a really strong jaw that you did not want to mess with. He was definitely in charge, but he was also a really nice guy. Bob and I didn't think he knew English, and so we tested him a little. You have to keep in mind that we were twenty-one years old, and as mentioned previously, the frontal lobes of our brains were probably not fully developed. We would say some things to him that were probably not very nice just to see if we could get a reaction from him. He acted like he didn't know what we were saying. So we kept doing that the entire trip. They weren't awful things—just off-color things.

We had breakfast each morning around 6:45 am before going out on the deck to work. It was the same kind of food every day and at every meal—at breakfast, lunch, and dinner—that high protein diet I already mentioned. To his credit, the captain had us for dinner in his quarters three out of the twelve or thirteen nights we were on board his ship. He told us about the history of the ship and about his career and his life and journeys around the world. It was really nice of him—something he certainly did not have to do.

Dinner was at about four-thirty or five o'clock every afternoon, and after dinner, the boatswain would

Adventure

Leisure time on board

lead us all up to the top deck of the ship where there was—believe it or not—a swimming pool. The ship had been built in the 1950s, and was not only a freighter, originally, it was also a passenger ship. Because of that, the top deck had about twenty passenger cabins and a swimming pool. A bar was also up there, and it was well-stocked, and free—great Scotch, beer, whatever you wanted. The bar was open every night and all the sailors were welcome to partake.

The sailors, by the way, were not what we had expected. They were all college educated and spoke good English, which made it easy to make friends with them. I believe one reason they were so well educated was that Norway's merchant marine sailors were not unionized. That was how Bob and I were able to have those jobs. We weren't required to be union members. In addition, oil had been discovered off the Norwegian coast, and the oil wells that sprang up were government owned. Every Norwegian citizen shared in the money generated by those wells. Our shipmates explained that that's what made it possible for them to take time off and travel around the world for a couple of years. They said they made as much as their friends who stayed home and took normal jobs.

We had a good time socializing with them at the pool every evening, and then, around eight or nine o'clock, we would retreat to our cabins.

The Canaries and Gibraltar

Having been on the ocean for twelve days, finally seeing land was a big deal. It made me think of the first

Adventure

The Canary Islands

The Strait of Gibraltar

American settlers who crossed in small ships from Europe and didn't see land for more than a month. It must have been a highly emotional experience.

When we arrived at the Canary Islands, one of our shipmates, who had been there a number of times, came with us and gave us a tour. Frankly, I do not remember much about that excursion, except that the terrain was very hilly and that we spent the night at a really bad hostel.

Next, we sailed through the Strait of Gibraltar. It is narrow enough that it was possible to see both sides at the same time—the Rock of Gibraltar to the north and the country of Morocco on the African coast to the south.

I recall looking over at Morocco and thinking that my father had been there more than thirty years before. It was where his involvement in World War Two began. He was in Patton's Third Army, the Tenth Light Artillery, and fought in North Africa, and then in Sicily.

One of the few battles he described to me in detail was about storming the beach at Anzio. He said bullets were flying everywhere, and his friends were getting shot, right and left. He said he could not figure out why he had not been hit, and decided to make a pledge that if he got through that terrible ordeal he would convert to Catholicism.

He did get through it, he did convert, and he even married an Irish Catholic—my mom.

After Anzio, my father was promoted to Master Sergeant and was put in charge of some troops. His brother was a bombardier in the Army Air Corps who

Adventure

The Port of Barcelona

flew out of Northern Italy to hit bomb sites in Germany. While my father was still in Italy, an officer came up to him and said, "Master Sergeant, I have a note for you."

The note said that his brother had been killed when his plane was hit over northern Italy. Of course, there was nothing my father could do about it, and so he just carried on. He continued into Europe with Patton and ultimately went all the way to Berlin.

Needless to say, seeing Morocco made me think about all that. It created a solemn moment.

We Arrive at Barcelona

When we arrived at Barcelona, the ship was forced to remain offshore, outside of the harbor, until a berth became available, and that would not be until the following day. So that is where we spent our last night on the ship. Everyone knew that when we docked, Bob and I would depart, and so the crew had a going-away party for us—which was really hospitable of them.

During the party the boatswain—the man we thought did not speak English—came up to us, and he said, "Jay and Bob, it has been a great pleasure serving with you on the ship."

We were shocked—his English was perfect.

He started laughing, and he laughed, and he laughed, until he almost cried. Obviously, he knew he was going to have a lot of fun with that reveal at the end of the trip.

Adventure

The next morning the ship docked, and Bob and I stepped on European soil for the very first time. I was sad to leave the ship, and our shipmate friends, but there were many more to be made and more adventures to come.

Part Two: Barcelona, Alicante, & Madrid

The City of Barcelona

Barcelona

The Port of Barcelona was a gritty, industrial area, and so the first order of business was to get out of there and into the city of Barcelona. We needed to get directions and a taxi, and we tried to speak Spanish, but that was a bust. I'd studied Spanish in high school, but it did not come back to me—except for a few words. But somehow we were able to communicate our needs. We hailed a taxi and were able to get across to the driver where we wanted to go—a hostel we'd found in a travel book.

That first hostel was rough. The word "shabby" comes to mind. It was in a lady's house in a lower middle class neighborhood. Frankly, I was a little frightened—I didn't know what we were getting into. But, as it turned out, the owner was nice. The place could have used a fresh coat of paint, but after a while I realized our accommodations were okay. It was clean. Clean sheets were on the bed. There was a clean bathroom. Really, we had nothing to complain about when all was said and done. We didn't expect to have luxurious accommodations. We were 21 years old, after all. We had backpacks—a two-man tent. This was like a camping trip. Clean sheets were enough—in fact they were great!

We spent a couple of days and nights in Barcelona. Nothing worth writing about happened, and so we decided what we needed to do was go to a beach resort. Barcelona is on the Mediterranean. There had to be a beach worth visiting somewhere in the vicinity, and so we did some research. We found one called Alicante

Adventure

Castillo de Santa Bárbara, Alicante

Adventure

that was about 300 miles south down the east coast of Spain. All we needed to do was take a train.

The train system in Europe was how we got around during the three months we were there. It was really something—at least it was in 1977. The trains were comfortable and almost always on time, you met nice people and could sit back and take in the scenery.

It was also easy to buy a Eurail Pass. Based on a Google search, today an unlimited pass good for three months costs just $761 for someone between the ages of 12 and 27. That means the Eurail pass holder can take a train at no additional cost to and from something like 40,000 destinations in 33 countries during the 90-days that the pass is valid. Of course, in 1977, such a pass cost a whole lot less, around $175 as I recall. What a deal! We could go wherever we wanted in western Europe—all we had to do was get on a train and show the pass.

Alicante and the East Coast of Spain

As a matter of fact, what stands out most vividly about that trip was the train ride, and not because it was a pleasant one. As 21-year-old guys on a budget, we wanted to save money whenever possible. Naturally, it never occurred to us to upgrade to a first class train ticket. After all, second class on a European train is not bad, at least wasn't bad at all on just about every train we took. An exception to the second-class comfort rule was that particular train. It was a fairly long trip that took overnight—a train ride that remains at the top of my list of uncomfortable situations I thought

The beach at Alicante

would never end. The seats were wooden—they were really hard and unforgiving. Imagine trying to sleep on an incredibly hard seat with a back that rose at 90 degrees. It was unbelievable—almost as if the seats had been designed by an unemployed engineer who specialized in torture chamber equipment.

But we made it to Alicante, a port city in Costa Blanca—Spain's south east coast. The capital of the Alicante province, its old town, known as Barrio de la Santa Cruz, has narrow streets, colorful houses and plenty of bars, cafes, and bistros. Other than the beaches, the big tourist attraction is a medieval castle, Castillo de Santa Bárbara, which overlooks the city from the top of a really high hill. We did not go up there but I'm sure it must provide impressive, sweeping views of the Mediterranean coast. All in all, we thought Alicante would be a great place to hang out.

The first thing we did was put on our board shorts—Bermuda-length shorts surfers wear—and head for the beach. It was beautiful—white sand bordered by royal blue Mediterranean water.

It only took a minute or two for us to realize we were totally out of place. Every other male on the beach had on Speedos—skimpy nut-huggers.

There were great looking women everywhere, just about all of them in topless bikinis, but we were fish out of water. It didn't take long for us to realize there was no way we were going to meet any of them. Too bad we didn't have Speedos to wear.

Later that day, we went to a couple of bistros, ate some good food, drank some good wine and found a

Adventure

Don Quixote and Sancho Panza, Madrid

hostel to stay for the night. We got a good night's sleep, and the next morning, we took a train to Madrid, which is smack in the middle of Spain—about 260 miles from Alicante.

Madrid, a Beautiful City and a Bullfight

Madrid is very different from Barcelona, which back then was a gritty, industrial place. Madrid is, on the other hand, a very classy and classic city—a beautiful metropolis. We checked into a hostel, and then we went sightseeing.

I am somewhat embarrassed to say that perhaps because of our underdeveloped brains, we did something I now consider disgraceful. We climbed up on a statue of Don Quixote and his sidekick, Sancho Panza.

An elderly man saw us, came over and started banging on the statue.

"Come down—get off!" he said in Spanish. "It's not respectful!"

Eventually, we did come down.

That night we went to a row of restaurants in an area of Madrid that reminded me of Georgetown in Washington—row after row of bars and restaurants. One thing I found amazing was that we could purchase a really good bottle of wine for about fifty cents.

We had a delicious dinner, and then we went to a nightclub where we had a great time. Eventually, around two in the morning, we went back to the hostel and spent the rest of the night.

When we woke up the next morning, we decided to go to a bullfight. Neither of us had ever been to one.

Adventure

Madrid

Looks like a standoff

Our plan was to leave late that afternoon and head over to Nice, and we figured we just had time to fit that in. We had breakfast and arrived at the bullfight about one o'clock.

As you can imagine, there was a lot of pageantry—men in costumes and women in period dresses. Trumpets blowing. The bullfighters—*matadores* in Spanish—marched in a kind of parade accompanied by the men, *picadores,* who helped keep them from getting gored by a bull. It was quite a spectacle—lots of cheering and clapping.

I was captivated by it.

We found our seats—the bullfight was about to begin, and that's when I noticed three young women sitting two or three rows down in front of us—two blonds and a brunette.

I couldn't take my eyes off them. *Wow,* I thought. *They're really attractive.*

Bullfights last a long time, and we had a train to catch. I wanted to go down and introduce myself to those girls before we left, but it was getting late. Bob wanted to go to the train.

I said, "Come on, we have time."

What followed was a tug of war that Bob won.

We left and took a cab to the train station where we got on board a sleeper to Barcelona. We found our compartment—it had three bunks on each side. I took a top bunk and Bob took the other top bunk—not knowing who else would be in that compartment.

As fate would have it, a family of four came in fifteen or twenty minutes later.

Oh, no, I thought, *this cannot be happening.*

I turned to Bob. "This isn't going to work. I'll be back in a minute."

I left the compartment, turned right and went into the next car.

You will not guess who I saw about halfway down in a compartment—the three young women we'd seen at the bullfight. I could not believe it.

I knocked on the door—they opened it.

I said, "Hi, I'm Jay. My friend and I were at the bullfight. We saw you there."

One of them said, "Yes, right—We saw you, too."

We talked, and after a while I said, "Is it alright if I get my friend and we bring our things here?"

They looked at each other, and after a short pause, one said, "Sure, why not."

Bob and I gathered up our backpacks, and went to their compartment. We had a great time chatting and getting to know them. I paired up with one of the two blonds—a young woman I thought was beautiful—an absolute knockout. The blonds were sisters from Canada. The girl with the dark hair was from Germany. She spoke English well and had met the sisters while traveling around. The three of them had decided to continue on together.

The train started for Barcelona, and after about an hour and a half, a conductor came into the compartment to check our tickets.

He was a young guy who could see that a party was underway.

I asked him, "Where can we get some beer?"

He said, "That will not be a problem."

The conductor left, and a few minutes later, he returned with a case of cold beer. Who knows where he got it—probably the train's larder.

So we drank beer and partied all night—including the young conductor. Bob became friendly with the other blond and the conductor with the brunette. We danced and sang songs—a lot of Elvis songs, for a reason I don't remember. We had a great time—a lot of good, wholesome fun.

As the hours rolled by we learned that when we arrived in Barcelona the girls would be going in the opposite direction from us. I recall standing in the hallway of that compartment as the sun came up. The window was down, I was looking out, and I thought, *I'm not going to see her again.*

It was unbelievable that after such a short time we would part, and I'd never see her again. As the saying goes, "All good things must come to an end," but it was much too soon.

Before long, the train pulled into Barcelona and stopped at the train station. We gathered our gear and stepped out onto the platform.

That's where we said goodbye. I was sad, but decided I needed to shake it off. Our trip had only just begun.

Part Three: Séte, Nice, Monte Carlo

Séte, France

We Think We're Headed to Nice

We boarded a train in Barcelona we thought would take us to Nice, which was about 400 miles to the east. After rolling along for a number of hours, around three or four in the afternoon—maybe halfway to Nice—the train stopped.

The conductor entered the car and said, "We are in Séte. Everyone out."

We just sat there.

He looked at us and said, "Messieurs, this is Séte. It is time for you to disembark."

I shook my head and said, "No—we're going to Nice."

"Not on this train," he said. "This is the end of the line."

He told us there would be a train to Nice in the morning—a little after 10 a.m.

We looked at each other and shrugged. We had no choice.

So we got off the train in what at that time was a small town, Séte, on the Mediterranean coast of France. We found ourselves on the platform of a quaint train station that resembled the one in the TV show, *Downton Abbey*. We looked around and realized it was a charming place that could have been the backdrop of a film set in the late nineteenth or early twentieth century.

We walked past a desk where tickets were sold and stopped at a line of lockers on the wall large enough to put our backpacks in.

Bridge to Séte

Adventure

We asked the person behind the desk for two keys so we could stow our gear.

I shut the locker, turned the key, and said, "Okay, what do we do now?"

Bob shrugged and nodded toward the exit door.

Outside, it was a beautiful summer day. In the distance was a bridge, which also looked like a prop from a period film. It was exactly like the bridge in the final scene of the film, *Saving Private Ryan*. It had the same curve in the middle—the same stones on each side—and it led into town.

We walked across that bridge and saw that there were plenty of restaurants and bars. Since it was a little late in the day to go to the beach, we decided to check out a small French bistro. We went in, sat down and ordered a couple of beers, Carlsberg, as I recall—a really good German pilsner.

We sipped, talked, and tried to come up with a plan.

After fifteen or twenty minutes, two young women walked in and sat at a nearby table. Needless to say, this drew our attention. Rather than be coy, we asked them to join us, and they accepted. They were from Paris, spoke English very well with great French accents, and were on vacation—staying at a beach house owned by the family of one of the two girls. I don't recall their names but will call them Giselle and Nichol. We talked for a couple of hours, had dinner, and got to know them. Giselle and Bob seemed to hit it off and Nichol and I gravitated toward one another.

Eventually, one of us said, "We need a place to

spend the night."

"No problem," one of the girls said. "You have sleeping bags, no? Why not sleep on the beach?"

That seemed like a reasonable solution—I'd slept on the beach at Nags Head many times.

I said, "Where on the beach?"

"There's a good spot not far away."

We left the restaurant, crossed back over the bridge, and got our gear out of the lockers. From there they showed us the spot on the beach—a good one. We rolled out our sleeping bags, and they joined us.

An Evening on the Beach

Giselle and Nichol remained with us late into the night, and we got to know each other pretty well. All in all, it was a delightful and educational episode that went on for two or three hours—until the time came for the girls to go home.

Before they left, we said, "Why don't you meet us at the station tomorrow morning before ten o'clock and come with us to Nice?"

They said, "Okay."

Bob and I agreed that if they were there at 10 am, they were going to go with us. If not, we'd have to leave without them.

Well, they arrived at 9:45 am, each with a suitcase in hand. We boarded the train, and headed to Nice—about a 220-mile trip past Nimes, Marseille, Toulon, and Saint Tropez. The scenery was beautiful and it was fun to share the journey with the young ladies from Paris, who were able to serve as tour guides.

Adventure

We checked into a hotel near the beach after we arrived. The time Giselle and Nichol spent with us was great.

Eventually, we emerged from the hotel, enjoyed the beach for a while, and then found a restaurant where we had dinner.

Looking back, something that stands out is how unabashed Bob's young woman, Giselle, was in public about how attracted she was to Bob. Every time I looked their way, it seemed as though she wanted to devour him. Nichol and I just looked at one another and rolled our eyes. This went on nonstop the whole time we were together. We stayed in Nice for a while—spent time on the beach—and then we went to Monte Carlo and toured around.

Monte Carlo

Monte Carlo is a beautiful city—palm trees, magnificent buildings. We saw the changing of the guard at the Monte Carlo palace where the movie star, Grace Kelly, who'd married Rainier III, the Prince of Monaco, lived at the time.

We had dinner and wine at the yacht club, which was incredible. There was an untold number of boats docked there, most of which were a lot larger than your average cabin cruiser. Besides room for an untold number of smaller yachts, the Monte Carlo Yacht Club has 26 "super-yacht berths" that are meant for crafts ranging in size from 90 to 200 feet. I'd say just about every one of those berths was occupied.

After dinner, we went to the casino, which was like

The prince's palace at Monte Carlo

Adventure

Monte Carlo

Adventure

The casino at Monte Carlo

something out of a James Bond movie—which one was it, *Casino Royale?* I believe so. As in that movie, at least 80 percent of the men had on tuxedos. Fortunately, the girls had appropriate dresses, and Bob and I both wore blue blazers, which got us in without a problem. I recall that I also wore my Nantucket red slacks. I was glad we had decided to bring at least some clothes that were a little dressy—the blazers and slacks had almost been an afterthought when packing. We seemed to fit in okay, and we even won some money. Not a lot, but it sure beat losing.

We Say "Au Revoir" to the French Girls

The next day, we went to the beach, after which we said goodbye to the French girls. It was a sad, sad departure—particularly for Bob who seemed to have developed a really strong bond with Giselle. We'd had a fantastic three days, but the girls had to return to their families at the beach house in Séte, and it was time for us to move on.

There is an epilogue to this story. We got each other's contact details. Giselle got Bob's home phone number. He wrote letters to her while we traveled to other places around Europe. Apparently, he'd told Giselle he loved her.

I'd sensed what was going on and had pulled him aside and said, "Dude, you can't lead her on like this. You cannot let her believe you're going to marry her or anything. It's not right 'cause it's not going to happen."

Bob said, "I know, I know. But it's hard for me to let go."

I said, "It's like me and the girl from Canada. It's not easy—I know it's not easy, but you've got to do it."

Much later, after we returned home, Bob took a job that required him to move out west. But he continued writing to Giselle—telling her he missed her and that she should come to see him.

We'd been home for about six months, when he got a call from her.

"Bob, I'm in New York. Please come and get me."

Bob said, "Oh, no—I can't. I'm way out west. I'm nowhere near New York."

"But Bob," Giselle said. "You said to come see you."

"Giselle, do you realize how far away I am from New York?"

"No—how far?"

"2000 miles!"

Bob had just started the job and could not take time off, and she didn't have enough money to travel to Denver. So Bob sent her to Richmond to stay with his parents. Bob's mother entertained her and toured around with her for a week.

Then Giselle went home to Paris.

Part Four: Rome, Florence & Venice

The Colosseum

Bob and I Travel to Rome

There were a number of life-changing adventures and experiences on this trip, and the visit to Rome is near the top of the list. We traveled there from Monte Carlo by train and had just passed over the panhandle and had started down the boot when something happened I will never forget. I was so exhausted at that point from our time in Nice and Monte Carlo that I leaned back as far as I could and put my feet up on the seat in front of me.

After a while, a conductor came by and started giving me a hard time. He spoke in Italian—I did not understand what he was saying but it was probably something like, "You cannot have your feet on the seat—no feet, no feet!"

An Italian gentlemen sitting nearby must have realized that I didn't understand. He leaned over and said to me, "He's saying you cannot have your feet on the seat. He says if you do not take them down, he can have you put in jail."

I thought, *Oh, my gosh!* And immediately, I took down my feet.

But the conductor kept on jabbering in Italian—giving me a hard time. This went on for a while. Finally, the same Italian gentleman sitting nearby handed the conductor the equivalent of about five dollars, and said something like, "Please go away." The conductor looked at the bill, shrugged, and went away.

That was just one of a number of hospitable gestures from Europeans that I experienced, and the first serendipity to take place on the trip to Rome. The sec-

The interior of the Colosseum

Adventure

ond one occurred with we met some young women from the Midwest on the train. We got to know them, and they teamed up with us. We toured with them for several days.

Among other Roman landmarks, I found the Colosseum to be absolutely amazing. I'm sure most people reading this will know about it—an oval amphitheater in the center of Rome, just east of the Forum. It's an elliptical structure made of stone, concrete, and tuff, which is a type of rock made of volcanic ash ejected from a vent during a volcanic eruption. It stands four stories tall at its highest point and could hold somewhere between 50,000 to 70,000 spectators. The tiers of seats were inclined in a way that enabled people to get a perfect view from wherever they were sitting. Construction began under the Emperor Vespasian in 72 A.D., and it opened under his son, Titus, in 80 A.D.

It is amazing how intact it was after two thousand years. I also found it fascinating to see how animals, such as lions, got into the ring—as well as gladiators and the slaves that fought them. There are trap doors, underground tunnels and rooms.

We took a tour boat up and down the Tiber River, which was an impressive excursion. We passed by a lot of ruins—aqueducts and so forth. It's amazing what the Romans achieved more than 2000 years ago.

After the trip on the Tiber, we had dinner at a nice restaurant, and the next day, we went to a number of museums and saw some impressive artwork and statues. But I will say that above all else, Saint Peter's Basilica and the

Adventure

A boat tour on the Tiber

Adventure

Saint Peter's Basilica

Adventure

Vatican City

Vatican—the papal enclave within the city of Rome—were nothing less than mind-blowing. I was awestruck by the paintings by Michelangelo and Raphael.

You cannot imagine the feeling I had inside Saint Peter's Basilica. Since I went to a Catholic school through the eighth grade, I had heard a lot about the Vatican and Saint Peter. Being there, and experiencing it firsthand, produced in me what I have to describe as a religious experience.

For anyone who may not know, Saint Peter's Basilica is a church built in the Renaissance style that's located in Vatican City. It was initially planned by Pope Nicholas V and then Pope Julius II to replace the original Saint Peter's Basilica, which had been built in the fourth century by Roman emperor Constantine. Construction of the present basilica began in 1506 and was not completed until 1626—a hundred and twenty years later.

Tradition holds that it's the burial site of Saint Peter, himself, who is thought of as Jesus' number one disciple. The word "peter" means "rock," and Jesus is quoted as having said to Peter, "Upon this rock I will build my church." (Matthew 16:18-20) Peter's tomb is believed to be directly below the high altar of the basilica. For that reason, many other popes have been interred there as well.

It's interesting to know that Peter's execution was ordered by the Roman Emperor Nero, who blamed Christians for the fire that ravaged Rome during his reign. Peter requested that he be crucified upside down because he felt unworthy to die in the same manner as Christ.

Florence

We Go to Florence

After Rome, we went to Florence—one of the most beautiful cities I have ever seen. By then, we were tired and wanted to take some time to rest, but that was not to be. When we got off the train, there was another train beside ours, and we had to walk across a ramp to get to the inner platform. When we arrived, we saw four young women standing on the platform. In a thick southern accent, one of them said, "Hey Jay and Bob, what're y'all doing hee-ah?"

They were sorority girls from school.

I said, "Well, hello, Sweetheart. We're doing the same thing you are—touring around, sightseeing."

"Where y'all stayin'?"

I looked at Bob—he looked at me. We knew they'd be staying in a nice place, and so I said, "Well, we're staying with you, of course."

We did stay together for a couple of days and nights, and we had a blast—at least I certainly know I did. We ate at great restaurants and drank inexpensive but terrific wine. We went to museums and art galleries and saw paintings and works of art by Michelangelo and many others. Experiencing all that was an eye-opener, and it was great fun to share all that with those young ladies from school.

Since there were six of us, being with those young ladies from school was like hanging around with our sisters. I have to say it was fun to have friends to chat with, drink beer and wine with, and to take in all the sights.

Adventure

Florence

Adventure

There's a lot to see in Florence—especially art, much of which came about due to the patronage of the Medici family: "The House of Medici" it was called, a banking family and political dynasty that arose during the first half of the 15th century. The family originated in the Mugello region of Tuscany and gained prominence to the point they were able to fund and establish the Medici Bank—the largest in Europe during the 15th century. Amazingly, the family also produced four popes and two queens of France—Catherine de' Medici (1547-1559) and Marie de' Medici (1600-1610). In 1532, the family acquired the hereditary title Duke of Florence and became nobility. Hats off to them for all the wonderful art and beautiful things they left behind for us in Florence.

Venice

Venice

We Go to Venice

Since we had Eurail passes we could go anywhere in Europe we wanted to go, so Bob and I decided to go to Venice. The girls frome school were headed in a different direction. We said goodbye to them, got on a train, and that's where we went.

It was too late to get a room when we arrived. Fortunately, we saw a group of people with backpacks. They were our age—we didn't know what country they were from, but we followed them, and they led us to an alley where all of us slept that night. Nothing scary or dangerous happened. There were probably 25 of us, and we figured there would be safety in numbers. We were right.

The next day, we found a hostel.

I guess I would have to say I was impressed with Venice, even though there was not as much to see inside buildings, such as had been the case in Florence, where there were so many museums and outstanding artwork. So we spent a couple of days touring around outside—riding along the canals in gondolas and taking in the sights.

Some people say they experienced a bad smell when traveling along the canals of Venice. However, we did not. Water was everywhere, and if we did experience an odd smell, it was the strong scent of the Adriatic Sea.

So many things about Venice are beautiful. St. Mark's Basilica, which dates from the ninth century, is remarkable with its gold guilt ceilings. Like many of the famous churches in Europe, St. Mark's is dripping in

Adventure

Saint Mark's Bascillica, Venice

gold guilt. The paintings on the ceilings are absolutely beautiful, and it is right on the water, which is really and truly amazing.

Venice is a beautiful city, home of Marco Polo, born in 1254, who was extremely brave and traveled the Silk Road from Venice to China for years. I'll bet he wished he had a Eurail pass and two French girls by his side.

There are magnificent homes throughout Venice. It's hard to take it all in two days, but we did our best.

Saltzburg

Part Five: Salzburg, Grindelwald, Germany, Norway, & Amsterdam

Villa Trapp, Home of the Von Trapp Family, Salzburg

Salzburg

The train from Venice to Salzburg took almost six hours. No hotels or hostels were open when we arrived late that evening, but not far from the train, we saw a man in what looked like a glass ticket booth. We walked over to it and stood in line behind two young women. It turned out that the man was in charge of a campground that was right behind him.

Bob and I looked at each and shrugged. It was a place to stay, and so we paid for a spot.

The man said to pitch our tent wherever we wanted. He also said there was a hofbrauhaus nearby, which made our ears perk up.

A hofbrauhaus is, in so many words, "a bar."

As you would expect from us, we struck up a conversation with the girls who'd been in front of us at the ticket booth. They were from Minnesota and attended the University of Minnesota—where they were cheerleaders. Can you believe our luck? I was beginning to think Bob and I were living charmed lives.

Both these young women had two things about them that immediately come to mind. They had pronounced Minnesota accents—"Minn - naah – sooh - taah." They were really fun and nice.

They followed us, and we pitched our tent near the Salzach River—a roaring, white water tributary of a river called "The Inn" that was said to eventually join the Danube downstream.

As far as we were concerned, the night was still young, and so we suggested that the four of us check out the hofbrauhaus. That turned out to be a good call because we had a really fun time. The place was packed with jovial people drinking, singing, and swinging around huge, overflowing glass beer mugs. It reminded me of a scene from the movie *Cabaret*. If you missed it, it was a flick set in 1931 Berlin during the Weimar Republic.

We drank our share at the hofbrauhaus

Adventure

Me and my Minnesota friend

We were at the hofbrauhaus drinking, talking, and having a great time for about three hours. Needless to say, we all got hammered.

We left the hofbrauhaus in the wee hours of the morning and stumbled back to the campground.

Suffice it to say that the young ladies from Minnesota were great companions, and we had a terrific time together. They toured with us as we took in the sights of Salzburg, which took a couple of days.

If you saw *The Sound of Music,* you know that the famous musical family that escaped the Nazis, the von Trapp family, lived in a beautiful house in Salzburg. Called "Villa Trapp," it is a castle-like structure that at the time we visited was a museum for the von Trapp family.

Salzburg

Adventure

It was something to see and had beautiful gardens around it.

It's interesting to note that after the von Trapp family was able to slip out of Austria, Heinrich Himmler [1900-1945] moved into their house. I'm sure you have heard of him. Second in command to Adolf Hitler, Himmler was one of the most powerful men in Nazi Germany and one of the main architects of the Holocaust. Rather than face the music after the war, however, he committed suicide by taking cyanide.

The Eiger overlooks Grindelwald

Switzerland and the Eiger

We decided to move on after a few days in Salzburg. The Minnesota girls were going west to France, and so we decided to check out Switzerland and the Alps.

The train from Salzburg to Switzerland was crowded. We were packed in together and lucky to find seats. Many of our fellow passengers had backpacks and camping gear with them, which indicated they were going where we were headed—no doubt to go camping and hiking near that mountain resort town of Grindelwald, which is known for skiing, climbing and hiking. Grindelwald, a truly picturesque place, is a village and municipality in the Interlaken-Oberhasli administrative district in the canton of Berne. Located 3,392 feet above sea level, it's a major tourist destination. It is overlooked by the section of the Bernese Alps from the Wetterhorn to the Eiger—a 13,015-foot high mountain.

Another Serendipity

By the time we got off that crowded train, I was feeling pretty bad—really tired—and I think I must have been coming down with a cold. I knew I needed to get some serious, uninterrupted rest, but the only way that was going to happen was to get a room at a hotel.

I told Bob that's what I wanted to do.

Bob said, "No, uh-uh, no way." He said he didn't want to spend the money.

I tried to persuade Bob, but he wouldn't budge.

We were on the platform at the train station having this conversation when an older man came up to us—probably in his fifties.

He handed me the equivalent of about twenty dollars and said, "Here, young man. Take this money. There's a hotel just down the street. Go stay there tonight."

I was flabbergasted. "How am I going to pay you back?"

He said, "You don't have to pay me back. Someone did something like this for me when I was young, and I want to do it for you."

I said, "Okay, thank you. I really appreciate it. I can't thank you enough!"

That night, I got a great night's sleep, and the next morning I felt a whole lot better. I was ready to explore the Eiger.

The Eiger

The Eiger is the easternmost peak of a ridge crest that extends across the Mönch to the Jungfrau at 13,642 feet, and it is quite a sight to see. While the northern side of the mountain rises more than 10,000 feet above the two valleys of Grindelwald and Lauterbrunnen, the southern side faces the large glaciers of the Jungfrau-Aletsch area, the most glaciated region in the Alps.

The most notable feature of the Eiger is its nearly 5,900 foot north face of rock and ice, named Eiger-Nordwand, Eigerwand or just Nordwand, which is the

An Alpine horn blower

Getting ready to pitch hay

biggest north face in the Alps. To get a good look, we took a train that seemed to go straight up one side, and then we hiked on foot for a while. Along the way we came upon a family and took some pictures with them.

I'll never forget that trip. We slept outside. It was cold, but the scenery was beautiful. Snow was on the ground in the middle of summer. We were so high up, in fact, that it was hard to breathe at first. It took some getting used to.

The boat we took up the Rhine

A hilltop castle on the Rhine

We Go to Germany

From Switzerland we traveled by train to Germany where we took a boat up the Rhine River. We saw one castle after another. It was amazing. Some were in good shape and some were in ruins.

We got off in Cologne. Originally a Roman city, Cologne has been around for something like 2000 years. Spelled Köln in German, it is a major cultural center for the Rhineland. There are many institutions of higher education, most notably the University of Cologne, one of Europe's oldest and largest universities.

Like other German cities, Cologne was almost completely reduced to rubble by allied bombs during World War Two. When we were there, in 1977, much of it had not yet been completely rebuilt, so there wasn't much to see—with one exception. Somehow the Cathedral of Cologne miraculously received only minor damage during the war. Its twin spires are said to have been used as a navigational landmark by Allied aircraft raiding deeper into Germany during the last years of the war, and that may be a reason the cathedral was not destroyed—the pilots liked having them there and so left them untouched.

There may also have been another reason. When we visited, we were told the spires were also used by allied bombardiers when Cologne itself was bombed. When a bombardier sighted the spires, he'd wait and until he was directly over them to flip the switch that released bombs. That way, the speed of the plane moved the bombs forward—beyond the cathedral.

Adventure

Another boat on the Rhine

The Cologne Cathedral

Adventure

What remains vivid in my memory about the Cologne Cathedral are the human figures carved in stone that adorn it. They aren't saints or cherubs or angels. They were just normal people from the time the carvings were done. Also, the cathedral apparently has a collection of the bones from holy people throughout the ages. They are known as the "Holy Bones."

The cathedral is the third-tallest church and the tallest cathedral in the world. It was constructed to house the Shrine of the Three Kings and is a globally recognized landmark—one of the most visited sites and pilgrimage destinations in Europe. Construction began on August 15, 1248 and was not completed until 1880. Apparently, the builders ran out of money every now and then and had to put construction on hold—in one instance for 300 years.

A photo of Cologne taken from an allied bomber during World War Two

On to Oslo

Norway Came Next

Bob's dad had a business colleague in Norway he had encouraged us to visit, and it was a trip we had agreed to take. The combo train and ferry trip from Cologne to Oslo took more than 24 hours. The most impressive part of that trip was the ferry ride. I'd been on a small ferry on the Outer Banks of North Carolina. That's how you get to Ocracoke Island from Hatteras. But the ferry to Norway was a spaceship by comparison—a huge, modern construction with restaurants, bars, and shops. I'd never seen anything like it.

The other thing I recall is that the land in Norway is very different from the parts of Europe we had visited up to then. It's very green, and of course, there are fiords—long, narrow inlets with steep sides or cliffs that were created by glaciers thousands of years ago.

We arrived in Oslo by train and took a cab from the train station to Bob's father's friend's house. It was a comfortable abode in the suburbs of Oslo. We didn't stay long. It was just Bob's father's friend and his wife. Their children were away at university. We had dinner with them—a really great meal—and we spent the night in their children's rooms. The next morning the couple encouraged us to go to a nearby amusement park.

People ask, "What was the amusement park near Oslo like?" I have to say, it was not what I expected. I've been to Disney World in Florida, and it wasn't like that. It was, for me at least, more exciting—more real. Perhaps "authentic" is the right word. For one thing, the people were very attractive—or perhaps "distin-

A marching band at the Oslo amusement park

guished-looking" is a better way to put it. Rather than shorts and T-shirts, for example, they were well-groomed and they dressed more formerly.

As you would expect for an amusement park, there were rides, and there were parades. The restaurants were good, and, of course, there were beautiful women and girls everywhere one looked, and everyone was having a good time. It was a carnival-like atmosphere—people drinking wine and beer, smiling and laughing. Even so, we did not stay long. We left that afternoon and boarded a train, a ferry, and another train to Amsterdam, which took more than 24 hours.

The Red Light District

Did Someone Say, "Red Light District?"

The Red Light District of Amsterdam is near the water, and there were canals down the middle of some streets, which were narrow and lined with restaurants, bars, and shops. Prostitution is legal in the Netherlands, but solicitation is not allowed out in the open. As a result, the working girls—practitioners of the world's oldest profession—display their wares by positioning themselves in shop windows, wearing really sexy outfits to show off what they have to offer. Some stand and others sit.

According to an Internet search, today, these girls earn anywhere from $200 to $600 a night—definitely beyond our price range, even if we'd been interested, which we were not.

All we did was window shop.

A Night in Amsterdam

After touring the Red Light District, we checked into a hotel, and then went to a nearby bar where we had a few beers and smoked a joint. That's right. Marijuana is legal in the Netherlands. You could back then, and you can now, get it in bars.

Bob and I were not big fans of marijuana, but we did decide to try a small amount. Nowadays, I understand that some bars offer a variety of weed from normal strength to "this will blow your mind."

What we had was the normal, 1970s variety.

We met some people at that bar and tagged along with them to a party, which was probably not a smart

Adventure

Amsterdam

thing to do. But it turned out to be a pretty good party, albeit different from what we were used to. There wasn't a band, but there was a lot of music—all kinds—hard rock, soul music, jazz. There were also some attractive women, but it was a different sort of crowd than we were used to. Punk rock comes to mind—Dutch punk rock, if such a thing existed back then. There were piercings—not just ears—but also noses, lips.

That was something I had not seen before

Everyone was high, but Bob and I were not. Well, maybe we were a little bit high, but we'd only had a small amount of marijuana. What was it Bill Clinton said? "I tried marijuana, but I didn't inhale?" If you believe that, then maybe you will believe that I inhaled a little—but not very much.

A couple of girls struck up a conversation with us. It didn't lead anywhere—not to anyone's boudoir—but we did talk for quite some time. They wanted to know about America, and we wanted to know about Amsterdam.

We asked them about the Red Light District

They laughed pretty hard and said, "That's our national pastime."

My impression of Amsterdam was that the whole city could be compared to a carnival—people out on the streets, drinking beer and wine, smoking marijuana, and having a good time. Picture Bourbon Street in New Orleans at Mardi Gras. It also seemed there were huge numbers of young people. I guess a lot of people were killed off in the war, and those who survived had lots of children. That's not surprising since the same thing happened in the U.S. The G.I.s came home from the war. They got married and had children, and the Baby Boom Generation was the result—all 75 million of us.

Eventually that night, we went back to our hotel. It was not an expensive hotel, but it was a hotel, nonetheless. The next morning, we headed for Paris.

Part Six: Paris & Dover

Paris

Paris When It Sizzles

We stayed at a campground just outside Paris that had its own train stop. It was still daytime when we arrived, and so we set up our campsite, and we went to find the showers.

The showers were good—there was good water pressure, and the water was hot. The toilet situation, however, left something to be desired. Basically, the toilet was a hole in the floor. You either peed in it, or you pooped in it. As a guy, peeing in it was not a problem—I could handle that. Pooping, however, took some figuring out and getting used to. I called it "the helicopter toilet" because I had to hold my arms out like a helicopter to balance myself.

But, what the heck? That campground was a place to sleep and the showers were good. At 21, who could ask for more?

Now that we were refreshed, we decided to leave our gear and head into town. By the way, it never occurred to us that our things might get stolen, and they never did.

We took a cab into Paris that day—it was not far or expensive—and went straight to that beautiful and famous boulevard, the *Champs-Élysées*. It really is an amazing street, extremely wide and lined with sidewalk cafes and restaurants. We had lunch at one of them and then checked out the *Arc de Triomphe,* located in the center of the traffic circle at that time known as the *Place d'Étoile.* Now it's known as the *Place Charles de Gaulle.*

Adventure

Place Charles de Gaulle, formerly, Place d'Étoile

Arc de Triomphe

That circle, by the way, has often been compared to the Indianapolis 500, and correctly so. Imagine hundreds of crazy French motorists all jockeying for position to see who can be first to get around it. If you are at a train station in New York or London, and you want to take a cab, you will find a civilized and orderly line of people waiting. Have you ever seen a civilized and orderly line waiting for a cab at a French train station? No—of course not. It's every man and woman for him/herself.

Now, imagine these same people with the same mentality trying to enter and get around a traffic circle.

We Meet Two French Girls

Bob and I were standing next to this huge arch, the *Arc de Triomphe,* when we saw a couple of attractive young women coming our way. Sometimes Bob, in an effort to meet young women, would go over the top.

This was one of those times.

He put out his arm, leaned against the arch and said to one of them, "Excuse me, can you tell me where the Arch of Triumph is?"

She gave him a puzzled look and said, "It, it's right here. This is it!"

And that is how we met two more French girls. They hung out with us for two or three days and showed us the sights. But it wasn't like the French girls we met on the Riviera. We slept at the campground, and they went home each night and met us the following morning.

Adventure

Notre Dame

Adventure

Here's a sampling of what we saw:

- **The Eiffel Tower,** which was built by Gustave Eiffel to commemorate the centenary of the French Revolution. It is one of the most visited monuments in the world and attracts nearly seven million visitors a year.
- **The Musée d'Orsay,** which contains more than 24 paintings by Vincent Van Gogh, including: "Starry Night over the Rhone," "Dance Hall in Arles," and "Vincent's Bedroom in Arles." That was something to see.
- **The Notre Dame Cathedral**—begun in 1163 and completed in 1345, it was definitely worth taking in, particularly its portals surrounded by many sculptures and the many gargoyles that adorn the roof. Unfortunately, it burned recently, but according to the French government, it will be rebuilt— which I expect will take many years.
- **The Louvre Museum**—the most visited art museum in the world was incredibly impressive—paintings by Rembrandt, Raphael, Leonardo da Vinci to name just a few. We could have stayed in it for four or five days and not seen everything there was to see. Located in the heart of Paris, the building that houses the Louvre is a former royal palace, with an area of 210,000 square meters including 60,600 for the exhibitions, including the Mona Lisa, and the

A cruise on the Seine

statue of Vénus de Milo and the one that

inspired the Rolls-Royce hood ornament, Winged Victory, known in French as *Victoire de Samothrace* in French.

- **We took a cruise on the Seine,** which is probably the best way to see the "City of Light." It provided a panoramic view of the Eiffel Tower, Notre Dame, Pont Alexandre III.
- **We visited Montmartre,** a hill located in the north of Paris, 130 meters high, which gives its name to the surrounding neighborhood. It's best known for the white-domed Basilica of the Sacred Heart, and of course, the famous cabaret, Moulin Rouge, is located there.
- **The Palace of Versailles** was mind-blowing—a huge complex of buildings, gardens and terraces, lavish decorations, furniture and gilded works of Renaissance art. The seat of political power in the Kingdom of France from 1682 to 1789, no wonder it's the most famous castle in France.

The time came for us to move on and we said goodbye to the girls at a train station in Paris and boarded a train to Calais. We were on our way to the United Kingdom.

Hovercraft from Calais to Dover

We Fly Ten Feet High to London

We took a hovercraft ferry from Calais to Dover, a service that existed from 1968 into the fall of 2000, at which time it was replaced by catamaran ferries that cross almost as fast but are able to transport more people and vehicles.

The ride on the hovercraft was a unique experience. You either drove, or in our case because we had no car, walked aboard and into one of two passenger cabins that flanked the vehicle deck. There, we settled into airline-style seats. The car hatches were closed and huge turbines lifted the craft about ten feet off the surface of planet Earth. Moments later, four huge propellers sent the craft blasting across the English Channel at just under 60 miles per hour.

We literally flew across the water!

We met an older couple on board—not as old as our parents—they were probably in their mid thirties or maybe early forties. They were friendly, intelligent, well educated, and they were curious to know what we were up to. We felt comfortable talking openly with them, I suppose because they seemed close to our age. They wanted to know about America, and they wanted to hear everything about our trip—so we told them.

We had quite a conversation going, but as we approached the English coast, I saw the white cliffs of Dover for the first time—which are truly massive and impressive. They really are as white as chalk—because they actually are, in fact, chalk.

Just after that, I experienced a sudden sense of alarm. The hovercraft was headed at high speed right

Adventure

The white cliffs of Dover

Adventure

into the coast and the white cliffs—but I should not have been worried. It made a seamless transition onto land and settled onto a concrete pad at the hover port.

By the time we disembarked, we were good friends with the English couple, and they drove us to London. They dropped us off at a convenient spot, and we hiked to a hostel where we set up camp. Then we toured around for a day or so and decided we wanted to see Edinburgh, the capital of Scotland.

The plan was to come back to London to see the rest of the sites.

To save money, because the Eurail pass did not work in England at that time, or maybe it was because we were idiots, we decided to hitchhike there—a distance of about 500 miles. We stood on the side of the highway for hours. Finally, to attract attention, we took turns sitting on each other's shoulders and hitch hiking, hoping someone would think we were funny and stop and pick us up.

That finally worked.

A couple, also probably in their mid-thirties or early forties, stopped and gave us a ride. The husband was a college professor, which is probably why they wanted to know what college life was like in the United States. They were easy to talk with, and we told them. It was a long way, and we talked a lot, but we also slept. The couple took turns driving.

Something else interesting I recall about them was the accent they had—a sort of a Scottish brogue. For a country that isn't very large—eleven U.S. states are larger in land area than the entire United Kingdom—

it has an abundance of regional accents—from Wales in the west to Scotland in the north to Yorkshire, to East Anglia in the East, and Cornwall in the southwest. Maybe it's because English was originally spoken only around London. At one time, those other areas of the British Isles had their own languages. They still do in Wales, although people there also speak English.

The couple took us about three-quarters of the way and dropped us off about a hundred miles from Edinburgh. We hitchhiked again, and it wasn't long this time before someone gave us a ride.

Part Seven: Edinburgh & London

Edinburgh

Edinburgh, Scotland

We stayed at a hostel in Edinburgh, which brings up some thoughts about hostels. For us at that time, hostels were okay. It was a place to sleep and to take a shower, but there was almost no privacy. It's a communal atmosphere—like being at camp when you're twelve years old. Everyone seems to get along, but Bob and I tried not to engage anyone at the different hostels, or to hang out or travel with them. We wanted to do what we wanted to do, and not to be held hostage to what others wanted to do. So we toured Edinburgh—in particular, the Edinburgh Castle, which took a couple of days.

Edinburgh Castle is at the top of a steep hill, known as Castle Hill, in the center of the city. It is one of the oldest fortified places in Europe and has a long and rich history as a royal residence, military garrison, a prison and fortress. When you climb up to it, you get a panoramic view of the city that will take your breath away.

Of course, we visited The University of Edinburgh, which received a royal charter from King James VI in 1582. That's the king for whom the James River in my hometown is named. The university officially opened in 1583, is one of Scotland's four ancient universities, and the sixth-oldest university in continuous operation in the English-speaking world. Some of the major figures of modern history are alumni, including Alexander Graham Bell, Charles Darwin, David Hume, and authors, Robert Louis Stevenson, Sir Arthur Conan

Adventure

Edinburgh Castle

The University of Edinburgh

Doyle, and J. K. Rowling, whom even young people will know because she wrote *Harry Potter*.

We also visited the St Andrews Golf Club and the golf history museum there. It's about an hour from Edinburgh along the way on a bus to Dundee. There's a bus stop at the St Andrews Bus Station, which is only a five-minute walk from the course.

The original home of the British Open, the oldest of golf's major championships, it has hosted that tournament 30 times since 1873—as of this writing, most recently in 2022. Currently, The Open is played there every five years.

One night we went to a bar at an Edinburgh hotel when a wedding or black tie dinner was going on. But the men were not wearing black tie. They had on kilts. That was an eye-opener—something I had not seen before. Apparently, that's formal men's wear in Scotland. The women were dressed to the nines—long dresses—they looked great. I don't have a reason to wear a kilt, but if I was of Scottish descent, I think I might do so.

We saw as much as we could in and around Edinburgh, and then, rather than hitchhike, we took a train back to London.

And that's when the fun really began.

Kensington Palace

Back to London

We returned from Edinburgh, checked back into the hostel, and toured around London. The first day we visited Kensington Palace, a royal residence located in Kensington Gardens, in the Royal Borough of Kensington and Chelsea in London. It has been a residence of the British royal family since the 17th century, and was where Prince Charles and Princess Diana lived after they were married in 1981. Currently, it is the official London residence of Prince William, now heir to the throne, his wife, Kate, Princess of Wales, as well as their children.

The Alabama Ladies

Good fortune raised its head again the next day—the last full day of our trip—when we were outside Buckingham Palace. We were there along with a hundred or more other tourists, watching the changing of the guard when Bob spotted a couple of attractive young women. He looked at me, nodded in their direction, and made his way to them through the throng.

"Excuse me," he said. "Can you tell me where the cricket match is, and when it's going to start?"

"Hell yeah, we can," one said with a thick southern accent. "We know exactly where it is, and exactly when it starts."

When I heard that drawl, I walked over and said, "You've got to be kidding me! Where're y'all from?"

"Alabama."

We struck up a conversation, talked for a while, and I gravitated toward one of the girls. She was full of life and fun.

Adventure

Buckingham Palace

Changing of the guard

"So how do we get to the cricket match?" I said.

"How do you get anywhere in London?" She said. "You take the Tube, of course."

And so we took "The Tube," which is what the Brits call the London subway, and went to the Cricket match. We ate fish and chips and drank beer—lots of beer. It was actually pretty funny because whoever put on the match that day seemed to try to turn it into an American style sporting spectacle—like an SEC college football game. At what would have been halftime, they had a marching band. We heard the Brits around us say things like, "Good Lord! This is so embarrassing! A marching band at a cricket match!"

We had a great time, which lasted about two hours, and then we had to find something else to do. None of us had been to the Tower of London so we decided to go there.

The Tower of London

The tour we joined took a while because there was a lot to see. A great deal of history had taken place in the Tower of London, which is no surprise since it was built by William the Conqueror, the Duke of Normandy who led his French army to victory at the Battle of Hastings in 1066—after which he became the King of England. The name, "The Tower of London," by the way, is deceiving because it's not really a tower. It's a huge, sprawling castle built on the north bank of the Thames. Its original purpose was to defend London from would-be invaders.

It was a really interesting tour. We saw where peo-

Adventure

The Tower of London

The Hard Rock Cafe, Piccadilly

ple had been imprisoned—not a pretty picture—and we also saw the nicer parts of the Tower, which have the atmosphere and feel of an elegant palace. The Crown Jewels are on display in what to me looked like a dungeon. There were stonewalls and wrought iron bars like you'd find in an old fashioned prison—maybe a 1930s movie starring Bela Lugosi. I had never seen anything like it firsthand. The entire trip was like that—a real eye-opener. I kept thinking, "I want to come back," and years later I did.

But that's another story.

The men who guard the Tower and wear Beefeater uniforms originated under King Henry VII [1457-1509]. They came to be called Beefeaters because they were allowed to eat as much beef as they wanted from the king's table. They still guard the Tower today and live there with their families. We saw their residences, and we also went down to the spot where the Thames meets the steps that go up to the Tower. It was something to imagine all the famous people who arrived there and ascended those steps knowing they would soon have their heads chopped off.

It was a comprehensive tour. We went all over, and it was fascinating. The girls liked it. We liked it, and we liked being with them.

The Hard Rock Cafe

From the Tower of London, we went to the Hard Rock Cafe at Piccadilly Circus, a theme restaurant with pictures of the Beatles and other rock stars, guitars and other musical instruments. The food was mainly burg-

The Grenadier Pub

ers, fish and chips—and not expensive, which was a good thing because by then we did not have much money left. We spent an hour or so at the Hard Rock, but the night was still young. Then someone suggested that the Grenadier Pub was a place we ought to see.

The Grenadier Pub

Secluded in a mews, which is a wealthy district of London, the Grenadier Pub was originally built in 1720 as the officers' mess for the senior infantry regiment of the British army—the First Regiment of Foot Guards—and was located in the courtyard of their barracks. It was opened to the public in 1818 as The Guardsman, and subsequently renamed in honor of the Grenadier Guards' actions in the Battle of Waterloo. One of its claims to fame is that the bar inside is the longest pewter bar in the world. We thought that was pretty cool and had a great time there.

Standing at that pewter bar, drinking, our conversation turned to World War Two. As I mentioned earlier in this book, my father had been in the War, and it turned out that the girls' fathers had also been in the War. Bob's father had been too young.

Well, an older gentleman nearby heard us talking. He came over to us and said, "I heard you talking about World War Two. I was in the Royal Air Force at the time. My children, who are about your age, are traveling around the Continent, just as you have done."

We talked with him a while about the War and what our fathers had experienced, and after a while he said, "Why don't you come with me for a drink at the

The Royal Air Force Club

Royal Air Force Men's Club? Have you ever been there?"

I said, "No, that would be great!"

He said, "Let's all pile into a cab and go."

And so we did.

The RAF Club

Located at 128 Piccadilly, The RAF Club dates back to 1917, and was originally called The Royal Flying Corps Club. What I remember most about it was the entranceway. There was a grand coffered ceiling with panels in it. On the walls of this grand hallway were portraits of brave young men who had been killed in the Battle of Britain. Each portrait had a small epitaph under it. One could not help but be impressed. It was as regal a look one can imagine—fine oil paintings in gold leaf frames.

We had a drink, and then the old gent said, "Ladies, I'm sorry, but you must remain down here—you cannot come with us. We are going to go where only men are allowed."

He took Bob and me upstairs, where the atmosphere was that of a typical men's club—an old world library look, dark mahogany, books everywhere, newspapers, and stuffed leather arm chairs. Men who had just come from dinner were there in black tie, having a drink. I was impressed to say the least. That visit to The RAF Club is probably what spurred me later on to join Richmond's Commonwealth Club, which has a similar look and feel.

Adventure

But like all good things, it came to an end. We had a plane to catch the next morning, and so we caught a cab and took the girls back to their hotel. We told the cabby to wait, so that he could take us to our hostel. But we found it difficult to say goodbye to the girls, and after a while, we paid the cabby and sent him on his way.

Nothing serious happened, just some kissing and no more, during our extended goodbye. We exchanged contact details for where we'd be in the States, and finally, at about 2 am, we returned to the hostel.

Big Ben

Part Eight: Home Again,

Home Again

My First Real Flight

We barely got any sleep that final night in London. We got up early and caught our Pan Am flight to New York. It was the first time I had ever been on an airplane. On the way across the Atlantic, I reflected on the trip and what I had seen. I have to say that, even today, the Louvre, the Vatican, and Florence are what stand out in my mind.

We landed at JFK, and then we took a train to Richmond.

Exhausted, I'd say we slept most of the way.

I have to say the trip to and through Europe changed me in ways that are difficult to communicate. Before I left, I was basically naive and inexperienced, but in those three months, I saw so many things and experienced so much that I returned as a totally different person.

A Hero's Journey

Joseph Campbell [1904-1987], a professor of comparative religion and literature at Sarah Lawrence College wrote a book, *The Hero with a Thousand Faces,* in which he discussed his theory of the journey or adventure of the archetypal hero recounted time and again in world myths. Essentially, he said that myths in every culture tell virtually the same or similar tale. A hero either voluntarily leaves, or is compelled to leave the safety and security of his normal, everyday world and venture into a realm unlike any he has ever been exposed to. There, he makes friends and allies, experiences all sorts of unusual situations, and of course, along the way he must face and overcome challenges. The hero who pushes forward invariably succeeds and returns home not only wiser, but in possession of a level of understanding and wisdom that elevates him onto a higher plane of being. I truly believe that is what happened to me—I went on what amounted to a classical hero's journey and returned home a different person. What I brought back with me was an understanding of the heritage of my European forefathers that resulted in a sense of confidence and sophistication that has served me well in all the years since my return.

Home Was Not So Sweet

Nevertheless, after all Bob and I had been through, and the adventures we'd had, I have to admit that it was somewhat depressing to be back. But I knew it was time to reenter the real world, and so I began looking for a job. I went at it full steam, but a month passed, and nothing materialized. Fortunately for my sanity, a girl I had dated at the beach before leaving for Europe returned home, and we resumed our relationship.

About the end of October, we were having dinner with her parents, and the topic of my job search came up. Her father said he was on the board of a bank and would give me an introduction. Not long after that I got a call from one of the banks top executives who invited me to have lunch. A few days later, I met him and one of his colleagues at a private club downtown.

Adventure

I thought they would want to talk about the bank and learn about my qualifications, but it turned out that they were much more interested in the trip Bob and I had taken to Europe. In particular they wanted to know the details of the encounters I'd had with the young ladies I'd met along the way. So, not sparing any details, I told them all about it. We talked for more than an hour about the French girls Bob and I met in Séte, the cheerleaders from Minnesota we met in Salzburg, and so on.

Finally, one of them said, "Wow, that is very, very interesting indeed." Then he glanced at his watch and said, "Oh, by the way, what do you want to do at the bank?"

I said, "Well, I was a marketing management major at college, and I also have a solid understanding of finance. It seems to me a bank would need a good marketing guy. Don't you need someone to go out and get deposits for your bank?"

They looked at each other and nodded.

One said, "You know, we do need someone to do that."

We talked for a little while longer, and the next day I got a call.

"Okay. You're hired."

I started at the Main Street branch, across from Bank of America, and ironically, I worked at that same corner, first at the savings bank and then at the Bank of America trading desk, for a total of 16 years. After that, I went to work at a brokerage firm and the rest is history.

Georgetown, Washington, D.C.

Epilogue

The girl from the beach and I dated for a couple of years, but eventually that relationship ended. After we parted, I went to a wedding in Philadelphia where I met my future wife. She and I had been dating for a while, but were not yet engaged, when we went to a cocktail party at a house in the Georgetown section of Washington, D.C.

We were on the balcony talking with some folks—I recall we could see the Washington Monument in the distance—when a woman I knew from Richmond came up to me and said, "Jay, can I borrow you for a minute?"

I said, "Sure. No problem."

I followed her down a hallway and around a corner, and there to my amazement was the young woman from Alabama with whom I'd spent the last day and evening in London two years before. She was working on the Hill for a senator from Alabama. It was fun to see her again and to catch up.

She looked great and turned my head that night just as she had that day in London. But by then, I had already made up my mind that I was soon going to ask my date, the woman I'd met at the wedding in Philadelphia, to marry me.

And that is what I did.

# # #

www.ingramcontent.com/pod-product-compliance
Lightning Source LLC
LaVergne TN
LVHW011840060526
838200LV00054B/4116